What Really Matters

The Hugh MacLennan Poetry Series

Editors: Nathalie Cooke and Joan Harcourt
Selection Committee: Donald H. Akenson,
Philip Cercone, Jane Everett, Eric Ormsby, Carolyn
Smart, and Tracy Ware

TITLES IN THE SERIES

Waterglass
Jeffery Donaldson

All the God-Sized Fruit
Shawna Lemay

Chess Pieces
David Solway

Giving My Body To Science
Rachel Rose

The Asparagus Feast
S.P. Zitner

The Thin Smoke of the Heart
Tim Bowling

What Really Matters
Thomas O'Grady

A Dream of Sulphur
Aurian Haller

Credo
Carmine Starnino

WHAT REALLY MATTERS

THOMAS O'GRADY

Th O'G

McGILL-QUEEN'S UNIVERSITY PRESS

Montreal & Kingston • London • Ithaca

Legal deposit second quarter 2000
Bibliothèque nationale du Québec

Printed in Canada on acid-free paper
Reprinted 2000

McGill-Queen's University Press acknowledges the financial support
of the Government of Canada through the Book Publishing
Industry Development Program (BPIDP) for our publishing activities.
We also acknowledge the support of the Canada Council
for the Arts for our publishing program.

Canadian Cataloguing in Publication Data

O'Grady, Thomas
What really matters
(The Hugh MacLennan poetry series)
ISBN 0-7735-1906-8
I. Title. II. Series.
PS8579.G735W48 2000   C811'.54   C99-901579-6
PR9199.3.O345W48 2000

This book was typeset
by Typo Litho Composition Inc.
in 10/13 Baskerville.

for Katie

Aoibhinn, a leabhráin, do thriall
  i gceann ainnre na gciabh gcam;
truagh gan tusa im riocht i bpéin
  is mise féin ag dul ann.

CONTENTS

What Really Matters

Quodsi me lyricis vatibus inseres,
Sublimi feriam sidera vertice.
           – Horace, *Odes* I.i.

DARK HORSES

Steady to the end,
the limits of his life
defined by fences, hedges,

headlands in a field,
he chose a day of rest
as if he knew the work

could wait, then sought
final comfort circling
square familiar corners,

sniffing for his brother
dark horse death. We
should pray for such grace,

that bred-in-the-bone
knowing what we're called to,
early on: plowing, poeming,

harvesting the sea. Would
that bareback rider raking
Irish moss at Skinner's Pond

agree? In my dream he clutches
madly at a white-flecked mane.
I wake when the anvil ocean bed

leaps up to meet the surging
sledge of beast and tide.

PART I

TRANSMIGRATION

Isan bhFraingc im dhúiseacht damh,
I nÉirinn Chuinn im chodladh;
beag ar ngrádh uaidh don fhaire,
do tál suain ar síorfhaire.

– Pádraigín Haicéad

I

Remember how we'd hike off every spring,
mother-bundled brothers striking outbound
streets like born-and-bred hobos just dying
to run away from home? Now we astound
our wide-flung selves to admit that once mere
names – Elm Avenue, Malpeque Road – could work
their exotic charm as far as Belvedere
and the last leg-wearying uphill trek
before the College bleachers. Then the race
to see who'd reach the railway platform first!
There, braced by a brownbag lunch, we'd all face
east, each year excited enough to burst.
Never, though, did our track-tuned ears detect
an oncoming train. What did we expect?

II

What should we have expected, standing there
at a whistlestop siding? Did we think
that just around the bend – the fixed point where
the familiar vanishes in a blink –
destiny could lie? If only native
wisdom had swung its lantern's guiding light
on that illusion – lent true perspective
to our final destination! We might
have been content to spend predictable
patient lives, as at home as the railroad
agent's wife who set meals on the table
timed to the minute the station clock showed.
Our grandfather wisely mastered the urge
to wander where parallel lines converge.

So. The cormorants have come home
to roost. Crook-necked upright bats,
I thought at first: Pictou Landing,
twenty years ago. Bagpipes balanced
on cabers. Unlikely twisted birds.

Now whole colonies host wherever
web-clawed perch, or purchase,
might be had: a half-sunken pier
at St. Catherine's, the pilings
of long-gone Hillsborough Bridge.

Misshapen blow-ins from over
the Strait. Brine-blackened sticks.
Why would I envy your more-than-
native wingspread ease? Wind-
whipped remnants of tarpaper shacks.

EXILE

Sometimes, exile makes the heart
grow harder than the iron edge,
exposed at last, of a long-discarded
cartwheel in the sand. The calloused
sole of absence, distance dulls
all but the phantom pain of taking
leave until I walk this stony
foreign shore.

At home the russet strand gives way
beneath soft feet except
where knuckly knots of mussels
barnacle themselves to salt-brushed
shelves of shale. Encrusted
so, not hardened to the core,
I suffer once more that surging bone-
deep hurt of parting. *At home. . . .*
Washed by that tide, my brittle bedrock
heart erodes.

So small that rain-besotted, wind-plagued place –
so shipwreck-shallow its surrounding seas.
Unmoored at last, cast off with derelict
concern, we swore to plant our masts – each sail
trimmed to a blazoned flag saluting *Life!* –
atop some lofty point of no return.

The thrill of risking all for a rich return –
hedging our bets, wagering that win, place
or show, we could find ourselves set for life:
how brazenly we held to that half-seas
over hope of catching fortune in full sail –
the blind-drunk dream of every derelict.

Already in our minds that derelict
coast, high and dry against the tide's return,
filled the horizon bright as a mainsail
spread before the four winds' will. Why not place
our trust in the billowing seven seas?
The way the delve and churn of Island life

dragged incessantly on, long as a life
sentence, who would dare judge us derelict
for choosing transportation overseas?
Guilt-free – knowing no jury could return
a verdict just to put us in our place –
with such giddy innocence we set sail.

Or ignorance. To watch those stormclouds sail
overhead dark as Fate yet for the life
of us never think twice that we might place
ourselves in peril – O such derelict
common sense! But how we spurned the return
of native wisdom, taking to the Seas

of Faith and Doubt like stars in a high-seas
drama of our own plotting, as if sail
and spar were actors' props we might return
to backstage storage, and our plight – true life-
and-death – was less real than that derelict
schooner ablaze in legends of the place.

Now how these heartless seas batter sheer life –
the salt-tattered sail of our derelict
souls. O to return to that harboring place. . . .

It is said that the suggestion of "Gulliver's Travels" came to
Swift from a returned Irish emigrant named Gulliver, whom
James Boies had found sitting in tears on the road to Milton,
and had helped return to his native land.
   – James Bernard Cullen, *The Story of the Irish in Boston* (1889)

Too good to be true, I thought:
that story of a storied figure's fear
of dying far from home

so like my own. Its wizened leaves
of wisdom clinging to a broken
spine – the tax and toll of time –

that old book seemed a novelty
(and that tale well told) until
this morning when I saw huddled

on a barren branch above an April-
swollen brook the unearthly gray-blue
form of a displaced soul.

O solitary heron! Today
I faced the stark image of my heart
grown sere in a foreign land.

Too late to be saved,
I must watch my words turn brittle
on the sapless bough of years.

SOUTH BOSTON PIER (1896)

after a painting by Maurice Prendergast

If only I could work in words
through time & space how
that wave of blooming
bonnets, plumed

fedoras, parasols – a Sunday
mass of color – splashed
so pertly as belles passed
in strolling pairs;

how smartly groomed
& sporting broad-brimmed
boaters, gents stepped out
so brightly in their wake:

how along the boards throngs
spilled until darkening faces
turned towards the sparkling tide.
Then I might tell

for sure what *eye hath heard*
& *ear hath seen* when
dreams lie dashed & a flood
of doubt pours in;

when shored up by heartsick
thoughts of far-off home,
a disappointed bridge
falls short:

when at last all hope is drowned
unless faltering bodies follow
a buoyant windswept sound.
Listen with me

now for how all grief sets sail
& spirits soar: look for the fiddler
bracing our sea-crossed souls
with airs galore!

I

So distraught I felt, for days afterward,
at the thought of our having gotten caught
in a scene straight from a 10¢ postcard –
Cattle Crossing at Argyle Shore. We bought
into it so gratefully – that vignette
of man and beast, a tableau vivant staged
as if to show how time's rough tide had yet
to mark the spirit of that place. Assuaged
by the pastoral – *genius loci* at large –
we savored with such bona fide pleasure
how an incidental turning (the urge
of *here!* or *there!*) allowed us to measure
an archetypal moment like purists
of "the Island way of life." Or tourists.

II

Tourists. Visitors. Company from away.
Fresh off the ferry from "the Boston states."
(So quickly wide-eyed wonder can betray –
as surely as accents or license plates.)
Outsiders. Blow-ins. Mere seasonal strays.
Who, truly native-born, could be romanced
as easily as that? *Rarae aves*
we seemed indeed (strange breed) until I chanced
upon nature's fact that the two-dozen
brown-headed cowbirds we counted that day
were hatched and reared in foster nests – that when
fully fledged they made their unerring way
back to the cattle-stalking flock: to *home.*
Really we had gotten caught in a poem.

Appraising the vernacular – those
    centre-gabled homes so native
        to this place – we drove like tourists

east then north along backroads
    red as rust. Past ditches rich
        with Queen Anne's lace, through

mauve-crested lakes of lupins,
    we trusted our quixotic common
        sense to guide us to that rumored

(not-quite-fabled) site – a fence,
    a field, a foursquare hut:
        the Island house primeval.

Stopping once to step off your
    ancestral land, a plot now lost
        to goldenrod and mustard

(how quickly weeds take root
    to fill out any vacant space),
        we stopped again to recreate

that pose my camera-wary
    forebears struck nearly fourscore
        years before: a candid shot

at Bear River station (my mother's
    father had been agent there),
        now ready to implode.

Tempus edax rerum, we took
    to heart (a hint of Ovid
        in the air) – and if not ravenous

Time then what devours all things? –
    until we stopped once more, at last,
        at that exotic structure:

a world apart, an age away,
    preserved as if in a photograph –
        even the central flue intact,

its mortared stone (no doubt quarried
    from that very patch of ruddy earth)
        rock-solid as the Delphic stump.

The birds themselves – skylarking
    kestrels, the first I had ever seen –
        seemed almost oracular

in their acrobatic flights of fancy
    script above that steadfast roof:
        enduring proof, we had to believe,

of how sometimes mortal work –
    a wall, a threshold, mortised beams
        (an image wrought in words?) –

can override what Fate has writ.
    Ecstatic creatures! Next morning,
        I found one dead of a broken neck.

LOCAL MATTERS

1 TRAFFIC

The way one ground its gears
making the grade below the school.
Or another shook the bridge.

My uncles had by ear the tune
of every vehicle for miles around,
& knew each driver's business too.

Coming & going. Except on Sunday
afternoons when strangers strayed
within their hearing's range.

"The Car Book" then! Translating
Who's Who by eye from dusty plates.
Local legend. Code of the road.

2 FORTY-FIVES

Five. Jack. Ace of Hearts.
Like saying your prayers.
Ace of Trump. High in Red.

My mother's done with Solitaire.
Low in Black. No reneging.
The rest will come back,

like lost words of a song.
Ace to my face. Dealer's trick.
Play down on the high man!

Local color, like reading a map.
Stuff her! My father's pulling
up a chair. We'll follow suit.

3   JIGS & REELS

Ever hear tell of a man who bet
the farm (& lost) that he'd make
the harvest moon itself mark time?

"To the devil his due." "He'll face
the music yet." "Bowing & scraping
as if to save his damn fool soul."

Or ours. With any luck he'll leave
us in his debt tonight. Footloose
& footsore before we're quits.

Pay the fiddler & call the tune!
Lord McDonald's. Fill Up the Bowl.
Local talent. Step to it, lads!

4   POST TIME

Hear how horse sense fills the air.
Or at least horse talk. Silks
& sulkies. Longshots & even odds.

Then feel how time stands still
for *two minutes flat* if you jostle
& jockey for trackside position.

I'll wager your heart picks up
the pace of pounding hooves when –
Win, Place & Show – standardbreds

make the turn & head for home!
John Willie Bob. Ventall Rainbow.
Local favorites. True to form.

5 AUGUST

Even a town-bred eye can glean
the season of hayfields baled
(or rolled) so clean that crows

complain of slender pickings.
Winter fodder. Can notice
how shortening days give way

to deepening evening dew.
Spring unsprung. Can read
at makeshift roadside stands

how all signs point to autumn:
New potatoes. Sweet Island corn.
Late summer. Local flavor.

Once, to mark the day
they drove the last spike home,

a decadent politician's wife
took the final mile – the ride

of her life! – in style, gracing
the cowcatcher's foredeck

like a siren carved
on a ship's curved prow.

No such luck for us that time
(April of '63) – our Zephyr

a wallowing blue caboose,
we followed a wedge-bladed

snowplow's tracks: so much
for New York on Easter morning.

Postponed. Stormstayed. Words
we practiced on the platform

at Port Elgin (a ploy to keep
us warm) speak history

politicians have disowned:
once, on a train route

now torn from the map, I flew
overland on a sailor's lap.

A FIDDLER'S SHARE

They'll pity you – *an idler's wife* –
& say "The dear, she'll have to eat
his words" & they may be right
that I'm caught in a corkscrew twist
of my mother's uncle's vice.

Maybe they'll recite the way
a horse that plowed back sod learned
to plod backroads & explain
how the lane's red furrows – fertile
wheel-wrought drills of clay –

would put to shame forgotten
fallow fields, or how the dawn air's
chill could cut to the bone
until you'd almost shiver & hear
reins fall from heavy hands;

then add, "His harrow the horsehair
bow he sawed across a gut-strung box,
he deftly filled his neighbors'
barns with reels & jigs, raw whiskey
& deep debt the harvest of his labors."

But I would have you think instead
of how, accustomed to that spavined
loose-shod gait – the sparkless tread
of hoof on pebbled loam – a swaying
couple rested beneath rugs spread

across a rough-edged tilting bench:
of how that man, my forebear, leaned –
head bowed to his hollow chest –
as the wagon's pitch & lurch led home
through acres he sowed, past fences

built to last; of how, her fingers worn
from kneading chords & stringing
lilting beads of notes from a beaten
keyboard sallow as tea-stained teeth,
the woman bore the fiddler's strain.

I think of the way her strong
sure touch once softened the ground
for a plot worked all night long –
of how you share the burden now
of an idler-poet's life & song.

An old soldier, my father's father,
survived the Kaiser's cruel juggernaut

(what were the odds?) to tell the tale
of how his regiment, the King's Liverpool,

decimated – the dead beyond all counting –
his good fate led him behind the lines

to a kindred band: farmboys, fishermen,
P.E.Islanders – helping, allied hands.

What were the odds that one of that small
company (his name now worn away by fame-

defacing time) had boarded the war-bound train
at Bear River station on the sort of morning

dogs love – especially a pup called Rowdy
who lives on still in local lore? The story

goes that each afternoon that forlorn mutt returned
to await his master by the disappearing tracks –

until the day the bad news came by singing wire
that another brave youth had fallen before that

rolling engine of death. *What were the odds?*
What canine sense foreknew the end

that no ordinary soul, and least of all
the railroad agent (my mother's father –

what were the odds?) uncoding that sad message,
indelible dot by dash, would dare to portend?

O what were the odds that fourscore years later,
I would page through his Telegrapher's guide

for some hint of how he bore up under
that burden of darkening doorways, grim cablegram

in his grip, and wonder if each casualty
left him as literally lost for words as I when

I heard of my boyhood friend – his mournful parents,
his wife, his dog – and could find only FULL STOP.

APOLOGIA

Not to the host of Heaven –
to thrones & dominions accustomed

to the music of the spheres –
but to the heirs & descendants

of a station master, his fever-
damaged fiddler's ear

attuned to the dot-dash-dot
key of vanishing lines –

the cricketing hum of pole-
strung wires,

the singing rows of cast steel:
to them I pitch my rhymes.

THE DEATH OF MILTON ACORN

They say "the melodious whistler," Jack Dale,
could charm trilling birds right out of the trees –
robins & finches, thrushes, chickadees:
a warbling chorus for his sweet-toned scale.
How they thrilled to his notes – some soft, some shrill,
as varied as their own in lilt & pitch
(some thin as the wind, some lavishly rich) –
until the day he died & the sky fell still.

What other way might feathered flocks mark death?
They say Milton Acorn would talk to crows
from a weathered bench in Victoria Park.
I swear that since he exhaled his last breath,
each summer evening the harbor air grows
thick with rasping gasps & the heavens turn dark.

Here. Where one day clay-soiled farmers
laid down their tools of mortal toil

like weary soldiers and walked away.
Where strong-armed Time now hammers

on its ringing anvil plowshares,
harrows, hayrakes into rust-red dust.

Here, in this unsown stone-strewn field –
mark my words – a poem stands

embedded like a gilt-hilted sword.
May it yield to the first worthy hand!

What shrewd mind designed this
odd contraption? Whose ingenuity
engineered these smith-forged

rods & pin-linked elbow
hinges, that trigger-driven double
crozier closing like a noose?

An anvil-ringing poet's, I suppose:
how else to hold at more-
than-arm's length safety those

cagey malodorous canine whelps,
priceless yelping pelts?
Black foxes. Silver-tipped pelf.

I

Hindsight may be beautiful. Looking back
through the froth-flecked teeth of those lethal jaws
(a marvel now unknown in Nature's laws)
about to lock fist-tight across the Black

Sea's strait, bold Jason – though rudderless – laughed
at how cliff-clipped feathers flew in the breeze,
grateful that even the Symplegades
might be outwitted by a dart-swift craft.

II

Looking back on what little I have wrought
toiling "hammer and tongs," a crude blacksmith
forging verse unfit to dovetail with myth,
I could cry. Hard-pressed as an Argonaut

by roiling words, their tide's crest high as ice-
capped peaks, my dripping oar an ink-dipped quill,
I think of mistaking for an anvil
a finger-enticing woodworker's vice.

Baited waiting. A line dangling.
The longing for concentric
circles in a pool. My father

knew the pull (complacency
of a Sunday afternoon)
of casting and reeling in,

casting and reeling in
(the fisherman's requisite
patience – a virtue rich

with its own reward),
in the backwater formed
by the hatchery dam.

I remember mostly
boredom, an enervating
ennui brought on by the drone

of insects – gnats, mosquitoes –
their bothersome presence
unrelieved by even

a dragonfly's elegant
touch-and-go. Did I learn
forbearance there and then,

in the entanglement of hooks
and filament, in the doldrums
of that far-off place and time?

Baited waiting. A line dangling.
Some days a poem seems as hard
to crack as that tight-hinged tin

of flamboyant thread-wound
barbs – hackles and yarn, fur
and feathers – buried (for when

all else failed) in the bottom
of his wicker-woven creel.
The anatomy of a lure.

To angle with words and rhymes
and measured beats. . . . The longing
for concentric circles in a pool.*

---

*   *Angling is somewhat like poetry,*
      men are to be born so.
     – Izaak Walton,
       The Compleat Angler

THANKSGIVING

Summers we'd give thanks to be city born
and bred when, come mid-August, our country
cousins trudged two weeks ahead to the stern
task of learning, the clean-cut drudgery
of school. Of course, in October we'd curse
the luck that gave them a fortnight repeal
of break-knuckle rules – though what could be worse
than digging potatoes in muck-caked fields?
Who, in their right minds, would envy that chore,
and pray – in late November, a thousand
miles and many years away – to restore
themselves by the grace of clay-coated hands?
Elbow-deep in a sack of unscrubbed spuds,
we swear never to wash off that red mud.

Each year, predictably
 as birds, or seasons –
  sometimes early,
   sometimes late –

we return to find the scene
 along our half-mile
  stretch of Island shore
   exactly

as we held it in our minds,
 its soul intact.
  If only our souls too
   could always feel

as whole as then, as
 thoroughly at home as when,
  surrounded by
   a quarrelsome choir

of gulls and raucous crows –
 the world's discordant chorus –
  a half-dozen
   great blue herons

strike their so serenely
    steady pose. How we envy
        such unstudied grace –
            their stock-still grip

in tidal pools and eddies,
    the undistracted gaze of
        creatures designed to bear
            precisely

the burden of their own calm
    waiting. What must we do
        to have our souls' weight
            lifted so, to make

the half-composed complete?
    What might dull the clamor
        of this crow-and-gull life?
            Last week,

on a mid-December morning,
    dying for home, we saw
        a solitary heron
            in full flight.

AUGURIES

No more playing blind,
casting about
as if miscast in myth,

seeking
in the feathered beat
of birds some sign:

today, ears cupped
to the August sky, we
eyed with awe

the northern harrier's
scouring scowl across
a fresh-cut field.

How the domestic
turns exotic
in a time of change –

the heron's croaking
homeward thrust;
the kingfisher's breakneck

plunge in a crested bay;
the osprey's taloned
plummet a sun-flung blade!

Once again,
midsummer's swooping loops
of swallows reduced,

resigned to lining wires
along the boat-bound
lane,

our last week
reads like a field guide
to the art of flight.

Walk with me now along this path,
this winding swath my brother cut
in a sun-stroked fit of morning

bliss – labor's love its own reward.
Our work lies ahead on a plot
of sloping hummock-thickened land

my giving father holds in trust
in hope that one day we'll lay claim
to a staked-out acre of home.

Home. How that ordinary field
has grown beyond all proportion
to mere survey-measured borders –

a scaled-down mapped-in sense of place –
until at last we know our task.
Like a newborn's parents, we have

our lot for life: Wild Thyme, Baybush,
Blueberry Hill? *Naming,* a poet
wrote, *is the love-act and its pledge.*

Some days, Paradise seems just a stone's throw
away; as easy, even, as the *skip,*
skip of a rock, smoothed by the ebb and flow
of rough tides, slung sidearm from a snug grip
across a blinking bay. One perfect fling
might send it skimming to the other side –
or so you like to think, imagining
its last beach-bound *hop* with Olympic pride!
Then how you would stride after it – a god
almost, almost walking on the water . . .
until, brought back to dry land by a *plod,*
plod in the sand – your shore-combing daughter –
you help fill a pail with sea-washed glass, boat-
shaped shells, and pebbles flat enough to float.

A poem leaves no more mark
upon the world than a gull's

dull cry at noon; or a gust
across the bay. Or the Point Prim

beacon blinking in a late-home
trawler's wake. What have I

to show for finding quiet
harbor here? Angel wings spread

on rippled bars, my daughters
singing *Echo!* off the cliffs:

a prayer makes time stand still.
A poem leaves no more mark

than whirlpools spooling thimbles
into rock at turning tide:

a fingerhold (and no more)
on a solid sandstone shore.

AFTER AKHMATOVA

Now and then the silence shivers –
a heron's croak above the roof;
the world could drum upon our door:
we would still play deaf.

VALEDICTION

I

The sea is not so calm
tonight.

This morning, as the tide
edged high against that bouldered
bluff that points a narrow channel
through the strait, we watched
a pair of herring gulls sit fat
as fallen skaters on a pond –
so sheer the surface lay.

Across the bay the island, too,
seemed more to hover than to float,
as if by breaking light a hand-shaped
cloud had brushed a tromp l'oeil
mural at the pearl-gray seam
of crestless swells and ray-
refracting sky. O how I wished
for the same deft touch to sketch
that scene inside an opalescent
shell: a fresco limned in miniature –
in shimmering aquarelle.

II

By noon, though, when at lowest
ebb the basin had drained to turbid
pools and shoals of mud-caked mussels
black as clotted ink, we noticed
most the ring of briny wrack left
cluttering our shore. More subtly
than that shifting archipelago
of terns we almost missed until
like wind-churned spray they lifted
and dispersed, the morning scape
had changed as if a scalpel-wielding
fist had scraped a luminescent
wash to yield – belied by palimpsest –
much starker tones of grief.

O for belief in auguries:
to see at dusk on our final night
that great blue heron homing – silent,
sure, a lambent form in numinous
relief against descending dark –
we might have deemed our own
departure true to natural design.

Instead, eyes shut, we listen
to the white-capped slap and slop
of rising surf upon the sharp-faced
scarp that lines our cove. How
could we, following portents, feel
resigned to setting out? Tomorrow
when dawn falters through an iridescent
mist, those cliffs – like ruddy cheeks –
will be streaked with salt.

PART II

BETWEEN TWO WORLDS

Jesus said, *"If you bring forth what is within you, what you
have will save you. If you do not have that within you,
what you do not have within you [will] kill you."*

– The Gospel of St. Thomas

You'd have guessed
    I was Gideon – the brash-
        toned bugler himself! –

by the breakneck fashion
    I pedaled that last sloped
        quarter-mile, deliriously giddy,

helplessly smiling (truly ear to ear).
    What had I to fear, what dire
        consequence of one-handed

steering, when with my other arm
    I embraced – triumphantly! –
        a brass trumpet encased

like the Holy Grail (richest of all
    rewards) against the marauding
        march of heathen hordes?

Heaven knows that's how
    a death-defying poem feels too,
        picking up abrupt momentum –

word by word, line by precipitously
    slanting line – as if on wheels.
        You've heard me speak

of that intrepid one-legged
        daredevil 'Kil' Kilpatrick?
            He took the Capitol steps

in classic style astride – true
        to its name! – a vintage
            "boneshaker," becoming

famous risking every other intact
        limb, wildly riding whatever
            was driving him.

One time besides I knew
        that brazen thrill myself
            of a rash breathtaking

downhill plunge – the morning
        I rode headlong from Aughavanagh
            in the Wicklow mountains

to Hacketstown below, hard
        bent on dodging sheep and cattle,
            potholes and pitfalls

on my steep descent. How I hung on
        for sheer dear life – the forlorn
            image of my unwed wife. . . .

(O horn of plenty – my unborn daughters!)
　　Now rhyme keeps my grip
　　　　on what really matters.

– St. Valentine's Day, 1997

METAMORPHOSES

si modo naturae formam concedimus illi

I

Three sisters stood aside & stared
as if, like prancing Pegasus,
their sire had unfurled wondrous
wings to soar beyond the gravity

that daughters grant to insubstantial
worlds. O how marvelous
that man seemed, their father
who with springing step had leapt

(what form!) upon that fabulous
machine – an untamed whirl
of spoke & sprocket, sparkling
chrome & constellated frame.

II

Such sport, such levity that flighty
feat inspired! Such festal spirit
I felt too to have that sorority
of ingénues admire the dextrous

way I dropped a softshod foot
(what grace!) to carousel through
corners like a coursing cavalier.
O how when I reared up & braced

to capriole the curb that bemused
trio – so demure, like maidens
drawing water in a frieze – spurred
me on my gravel-strewn career!

III

How then could I – like Ixion, head
high in a cloud! – predict their fright
when still astride that steel-pedaled
steed I peeled my shirt, unbillowed

to a sweat-bedappled pelt, & bade
their mother mount, side-saddle,
the horizontal bar & ride?
(What gall!) Had Hippodamia wed

the Centaur would she have heard such
grief? *O unbridled double nature!*
She sent me spinning & that coy
trinity sighed in high relief.

SAFETY POINTS

While a man rests on a space in which there
is a small circle, it cannot be captured.
                              – How to Play Parcheesi

Little do they know, my daughters,
puzzling over an arcane rule
of an archaic game unboxed
to pass a rainy afternoon:
sometimes life is utterly cruel.

So be it. For now, they have formed
their own small circle by the fire,
a secure world unto itself
where all that matters – that place set
apart – matches the heart's desire.

A *Safety Point* in fact, I think,
its rough geometry precise
enough – a measure of childhood
innocence – to weather even
the random roll of fickle dice.

Or the luck of the draw. Or Dame
Fortune's wheel spun to the helter-
skelter pace of the daily round.
By what fair chance might I find rest
in a space which grants such shelter?

So be this too – that circle squared
by the sum of fatherly math,
an odds-defying algebra,
the law of storm and stress: *A man
cannot be captured on the Home Path.*

To think that all that time we blamed the spite
of our neighbors – a rabid, demented
pack of God-forsaken, fiend-tormented
curs (though more bark behind our backs than bite) –
on that dismembered Christ, *sans* crucifix,
I unearthed in the garden our first month there,
piercing its heart with the rake's cruel spear:
one of my weekend centurion's tricks.

Jesus wept! If only we had known how
jackals sense calamity in the air –
hovering pestilence, flood, famine, drought:
our fault to have overlooked that horseshoe
hanging wrongside up I found our seventh year.
We left before our luck had all run out.

THE MIRACLE

Time's livid final flame leaps
and, in the following darkness,
ruin of all space, shattered glass
and toppling masonry.

It's not what Haydn sought
at the grand finale but what he found
when turning around
to face the press of hot-

blooded bodies about
to be flattened by that chandelier:
how they staved off Fate by ear,
without a moment's doubt.

What if, against all reason, rhymes
could thwart that fickle thief
and move us to contend
with our age's falling light? Sometimes
hearing is believing. Belief
is still what saves us in the end.

Take *It Don't Mean a Thing*
as one instance – the version
from '35, with Django swinging

with such reckless insouciance
over brother Joseph's pulsing banjo-
esque chords, the two of them free

as a pair of gypsies (which they were).
Hear what I mean about Stéphane's
breathing rarefied air – as if

in some other life he had seen
fearless Egyptian engineers
scaling scaffolds on the first

of the World's Seven Wonders
and thought *how much like rappelling
to improvise lines on the violin?*

Once he unraveled his art's
dark secrets: "It is a mystery,
like the pyramids."

Capriccioso. Capricious as the devil,
if half the tales his devotees tell

ring with even a crooked crotchet
of gospel truth. My favorite

one of all makes Nero turn over
with envy in his grave (wherever

that high-strung fiddler, immodest
to the end – *What an artist*

the world is losing in me! –
may lie): the time in London he

taught an entire orchestra
how to play with fire. *Scordatura.*

Pizzicato. Trills. Harmonics.
Multiple stopping. All the tricks

in the book! And every demi-
semiquaver so dazzlingly

right on cue that no awestruck,
dumbfounded blameless mortal took

note of how minor parts succumb
to a guttering music-desk flame.

Give old Niccolò his due:
for such a gift, by God, I too

would sell my soul at any price.
Il Maestro's forte – no caprice –

like a candle burns just once.
Call it *sprezzatura*: nonchalance.

1 "THEY BECAME MERMAIDS"

The wet centre is bottomless.

Local legend has it how, beleaguered
by a frothing mob of pent-up gallants –
brothers, uncles, cousins, all with talents
of a cutthroat sort, a bold *avant-garde*
hard bent on making right a sordid wrong –
a sorcerer asked his abducted bride
would she take the plunge. How could she decide?
To which dark camp would she rather belong?
The story goes that the cold wizard swept
her into the lake's unfathomable heart,
down a churning channel drawn on no chart,
out to the open sea. I think she leapt.
Tales tell of a seal-like pair basking bare
on the rocks: sometimes they come up for air.

Learning (they say) is a light burden; from
what little I've learned over time, marriage
too may be borne like any other sum
or substance worth its own weight. By carriage,
trundle cart, or barrow we transport goods
to here and there; by wagon, truck or train –
bridging rivers, traversing tangled woods
by elevated track or rutted lane –
freight rolls along, no more cumbersome a load
than what that couple on that bright tandem
in the song distributed as they rode:
life's cargo squared, not conveyed at random.
Love (I've learned) is an axle made of steel:
every morning reinvent your wheel.

Never build a marriage like a nine-mile bridge –
engineering pre-fabricated parts,
trusting trestled feet sunk by a delving dredge
(drafted first to scale on blueprinted charts)
can truly withstand the stress of ice-packed
seas and the mass of a steel-girded bed
on top. God knows how time and tide exact
their tax and toll on whatever sits dead
in the water – how all that will endure
sails free of conformity and fixed notions,
like that rigged-out schooner ablaze offshore
in local lore: a phantom of the oceans.
Make marriage burn like a ship spurning land:
weigh anchor, link by link, hand over hand.

THE ORIGIN OF SPECIES

We will now discuss in a little more
detail the struggle for existence.

Consider, for example, that oddly-
roofed species of an outbuilding behind
our house – proof positive (at least to my mind)
of how all things undergo ungodly
change. Now a mere glorified garden shed,
years ago it held a horse-drawn carriage;
then, expanded to a full-size garage,
a Pontiac long and sleek as a sled.

We should take heart. If ever over time
love's well-worn floorboards start to sag (despite
due care), beams bend, walls lean, be not unnerved:
fittingly, that which evolves survives – no crime
against nature; and on these grounds, *each slight
variation, if useful, is preserved.*

Insomnia. Homer. Sails billowing
like sheets torn from the shipping news of Troy,
the Hellenic fleet a flock of white cranes

holding steady course for shore. Anxious joy
I read behind those lines from a poet
who professed high faith in unfettered words,

their wide wings spread across the winedark sea.
Praise metaphor! And praise majestic birds.
But heed how even the Achaeans knew

that love alone sets the world in motion.
Homer may nod. Love – restless, unpillowed
love – plays deaf against the surging ocean.

RUSSIAN WEDDING

after Chagall

Call it what you will –
       old-fashioned, anachronistic,
             over-the-hill;

still there's something
       to be said when even
             the leaning houses

have eyes for a strolling
       bride & the whole world
             of shouldered bundles,

yoked buckets, balanced
       baskets stops in its tracks
             before the fiddler's bow:

life in equilibrium, poised
       on the brink of years!
             The poet, hoisting a toast,

brings up the rear. . . .

All summer, some species of blight or mite
has been killing our trees. The young maples
seem hardest hit (or bit), their leaves falling
like flakes of rust from the undercarriage
of an old truck abandoned in a field.
The slightest breeze, even the trifling weight
of a squirrel leaping branch to branch, shakes
down crackling torrents, late spring's forty shades
of greenery turned to brittle husks. Soon
the backyard will be bare before its time.

We have heard of marriages crumbling just
that way, the verdant canopy of love
growing thinner hour by hour as if shot
through – root to bole to bending bough – by rot.
Insidious disease or gnawing pest!
Looking up into those tattered remains,
we half-imagine strained heartstrings breaking
like twigs snapped from an overarching bower –
and wonder: is there no defense against
this spiteful bane, this life-devouring scourge?

Is there no known remedy – no physic,
no sure cure – to reverse this lethal curse?
None, we learn, beyond its natural course.
Or beyond the hope we take wherever
it may blossom. Cupid, legend tells us,
fashioned his trusty bow from a *bois d'arc* –
a brushwood hedge – like that barren bush
that once bowed gracefully along our fence.
We note how the jasmine honeysuckle
presumed long-dead now bears a second bloom.

Some still prefer to use *dot* (rhymes with *got*),
a loanword from the French – *dot* (rhymes with *go*) –
when referring to what a bride once brought
to a new union; not just her *trousseau* –

two settings of fine china, a hope chest
stuffed with cross-stitched linens – but *real* chattel:
four fertile fields, turf-rights to the best
half-rood of bog, a few head of cattle. . . .

At worst, the *dot* might seal a legal pact,
add final punctuation as an end
in itself: a match made matter-of-fact,
a deal approved on grounds of make-pretend.

Sometimes, though, it paved way for the future.
Take that woman from slab-rich Liscannor:
her wedding day a point of departure,
she founded marriage on a flagstone floor.

– Limerick, July 1998

EAST SIDE STORY

I

Holding at forearm's length
an old recording, its coalhard burnish
sheer as pearls of jet, I can almost divine
that 'thirties world of East Side
walkups: lace-ruffled curtains,
heavyset sofas, doilies,
dark veneer –

my father's place and time.

Like a prayer (or like a charm)
a thumb-rubbed label – *Miss McLeod's,*
The Bard of Armagh, Bing's *Without a Song* –
can almost conjure up his father
ushering Sunday-collared countrymen
to square-backed chairs half-circled
in a line.

II

It lent the parlor focus,
like a shrine. Or like a hearth.

Or like the gilded ark from *Exodus*.
Though common as a steamer trunk upended deep
in steerage, taking space, that Edison Victrola
seemed a cubit-measured casket for plates
of black shellac encased in upright
shelves below the crank-wound works.
Tempered tablets etched in finespun
whorls like fingerprinted code, those
waxen disks composed a tabernacled
covenant for homesick exiles
fixed in heartsore hope before
the upraised lid.

That phonograph: its corner
was the center of the room when
my father, from the doorway, watched
in wonder as his father touched the stylus
to a well-worn groove. Then how
those sea-crossed bodies moved!
Delivered by the lilt or swing
of John McCormack, Michael Coleman –
Goodman's *Sing, Sing, Sing* –
transplanted neighbors, cousins,
friends all linked uplifted hands
to bind their newfound land of promise
with one now left behind.

III

Witness to that test (or testament)
of trust, my father told this story less
like memoir than like myth, as if familial
fact meant more as tribal lore of rustic rites.
And yet the tableau that he sketched
seemed so temporal at heart: not epic
but nostalgic, his self-effacing art
restored to truest life the moment
when – between two worlds – a father
turned toward his son as if familiar
tunes and tones could summon
the spirit of longlost
place and time.

Holding at forearm's length an old recording,
I can almost feel my father's father link
his hand with mine.

THE TEST OF THE BOW

Remembering Michael Coleman

Before he faced the suitors in the hall,
He proved himself by plucking high-strung gut
Until it hummed a single note. So pure
It sang – a ringing, feathered bolt of sound –
That even brazen bucks (their noisy brawl
An antidote for doubt) fell still; around
The walls skirts quivered for the first strong cut,
The larksome thrill of severed air.
                       So sure,
Then, one man stood above this throng, elbow
Arced, fingers poised to throw them into thrall.
What goddess nodded portent from the door?
He bowed toward his muse, that blood should flow:
Brash bodies moved, then shoved to fill the floor.
He proved himself the master of them all.

AFTER LOOKING INTO R. J. O'DUFFY'S
*HISTORIC GRAVES IN GLASNEVIN
CEMETERY* (1915)

– Let us go round by the chief's grave, Hynes said. We have
time.

I

We had time that day, Dublin's high noon sun
conspiring at every turn to recast

classic forms, to play like mutating shadows
on the winding sheets of tarmacadam,

gravel, dirt: my Aeneas to your Virgil
to my Dante – back and forth in the land

of the dead. Father and son, we took heart
against the heat at Parnell's ivy-bordered

bower, almost marveling that no guardian
strained to roll away the stone, the quarried

mass a praying people laid out to atone
for mortal guilt: the weight of a great man gone.

II

Gone but not forgotten, we left unsaid,
not daring to name the specter of our own

dark end: with what utter finality
ordinary lives recede. Today, a book

returned me to that sweltering hour spent
searching through the patternless warp and weft

of paths for a spot we called *the weaver's grave,*
a short-lived writer's plot – to how we shivered

there, worn viators, in the sheer candescence
shimmering off the bleached unseeded clay:

how our stunted shadows seemed to unravel
to bleary shades of gray, then disappear.

– Colum

I

Still forlorn after weeks,
still reeling from exile's
first slap, the sting of salt-
licked rain off Dublin Bay

across my sorrowful cheeks,
I sickened at how all
near to me, oceans away,
slept on while I – as if

dead to that world – walked
thronging foreign streets
& dreamt of swift return:
if only for one day.

II

"It's only for a year,"
I wrote to lessen longing.
My mother wrote of weather
in reply until lost in the ache

of being neither here
nor there, I almost broke
with hunger for the scent
of line-dried laundry starched

by early frost – so real
& yet so unreachably far
from where I spent each
waking, or wakeful, hour.

III

How I lived for letters
filled even with old scraps
of news – page after transporting
foolscap page of local names,

familiar places ... *life*
in short, until that morning,
my sloven's hair grown
long by monkish self-

neglect, I read that word
my mother's mother's
mother used to tease
a sheepishly untonsured son:

IV

streelish, she spelled it –
from *straoille* (I had learned)
in the native Doric
meaning "untidy crone."

O what would I give
now – unfathomable depths
& graying decades hence –
for how those doubly crossing

syllables lifted me, freshly
shorn & fit for the fold,
from an *An Lár* barber's throne?
O to feel so suddenly at home.

Coincidence. How a poem begins.
(Or how it ends.) A convergence of word
and deed bound to the poet's need to hunt
out of mundane event or rare (or rare
enough) occurrence a potent force field:
the plain made strange, the odd matter-of-fact.

This is a poem grounded on firm fact:
Julianstown, Co. Meath (so it begins),
late July, the dawn air clean as a field
of freshly threshed corn (the generic word
for grain in those parts) – a dazzlingly rare
start to an Irish day. "Perfect to hunt

snipe," I muse aloud ... though I do not hunt
prey – birds or beasts – of any stripe; in fact,
when I think even of fishing (a rare
outing in my youth), my stomach begins
to churn in regret. ... *Snipe*: the very word
for a small fowl camouflaged in a field –

so on my morning walk I scan each field
with eyes unaccustomed to such a hunt.
What I observe instead – not quite the word
made flesh – is a snipe-rousting dog (a fact
of bucolic life) ... and my mind begins
to look ahead by looking back at a rare

rash act: how we just bought one of that rare
(in our parts) breed, a pup born for such field
work. . . . So I ask: "Her time with us begins
in one week – what if she expects to hunt?"
Springer spaniels (this is a well-known fact)
live to flush out game – unfortunate word –

and with one neat leap they can (in a word)
"spring" hapless creatures from their nests. A rare
spectacle indeed, I grant . . . but the fact
remains that I find the ethos of *Field*
& Stream (for example) – the call to hunt
and kill – unconscionable. . . . Thus begins

an event-made-word; now Hutchinson's Field
hosts a rare sight – a springer on the hunt.
This poem, in fact, ends where it begins.

Time devours all things,
I read in a book. But that night
I heard my second cousin

still a din-filled pub outside
Kilbeggan – his perfect tenor
pitch the charm – I took great heart.

The Fields of Athenry he sang,
every body there transfixed
(transported, too, by that tale

of love's promise thwarted
by pitiless laws) as if the gnawing
fang, the grinding jaw of minutes,

hours – ravenous years! –
had surrendered to a potent spell:
as if enchanted words could help

us dwell forever far beyond
that cavernous maw. As if
in the end, our slates wiped clear,

we might hold at bay the beast
by the door: the barman's "Time,
gentlemen, time; no more!" –

his "Drink up now, the Guards
are drawing near. No need to go
home, but you can't stay here."

CLOSE TO DEATH

I EARLY

This morning I rose earlier even
than that proverbial worm-prudent bird;

but not for fresh bait (despite what I've heard
about dawn and the elusive Salmon

of Knowledge). I got up to cast my eye –
hook, line, bobber and lead sinker – across

the froth-topped turbulence of recent loss
toward calm concentric ripples in the sky.

By that gray pool, I thought, that windowpane
on the deep, deep heavens – in that last breath

before light plunges through the murky depth
(as if Reason's lucid reach could explain

what lurks beneath the surface of our night) –
solace might emerge with the rhythmic *flick,*

flick of an angler's wrist or the pulse-quick
fluttering of the day's first flock in flight.

Again last night. That dream of a grown man
in the throes of silent woe for a dog,
mistaken by a neighbor for a sheep-
marauding beast, shot dead. My mother's father.
Can such inexpressible sadness span
generations, dormant until some jog –
some hurt – frees a memory bred marrow-deep
in the bone, one wound opening another?

Give sorrow words, sage Malcolm urged Macduff,
warranting outspoken pain its own relief,
raw anguish bandaged by a frank-tongued art.
Could one such poem ever be enough
to assuage a stricken soul? Or is grief
congenital like a hole in a heart?

What was I thinking that night
I clambered through the paneless
barn window, out of breath at the news?

Ground swell gripped the heavy
doors, sheer weight like stone slabs
sealing a chambered vault,
somewhere deep inside the stiffening
corpse of the family dog.

So close to death I felt as I knelt
by that laid-out form, thrilled to stroke
the silken flank, still life-warm. . . .

And yet so far from what I knew
next morning, our two cats circling
the vacant corner by the kitchen flue,
an empty space.
                    All last night
I thought of walking around and around
a cold plot, a swollen mound of newly-
heaved clay, a pain-broken place.

I could be tempted, Love, in times like these
afflicted by such worldly cares. Struck blind,
unable to see the forest for the trees

branching out like a virulent disease –
light snarled with darkness, day & night entwined –
I could be tempted, Love. In times like these

we feel for the hound-flushed hare as it flees
through the thicket, hearing the beast's jaws grind,
unable to see the forest; for the trees –

life's undergrowth – have overrun our knees,
our hearts, our heads! Already half-inclined,
I could be tempted. Love, in times like these,

still blazes the serpentine trail that frees
entangled souls – thorn-tormented, resigned,
unable to see. . . . The forest (for the trees

cluster so close) whispers how we should seize
what fruit hangs here & leave this copse behind.
I could be tempted, Love, in times like these,
unable to see the forest for the trees.

AFTER VIEWING DAVID BLACKWOOD'S
LOST PARTY AT SEA: THE SIGN

Where, they must have asked
    forever afterward, as I do now –
        Where in God Almighty's name –
    had anyone seen or heard before
a bird of such unnerving portent?

Never in all my *de profundis* days
    and nights spent shaking
        in frozen fear of Death –
    not even in my wildest, *wildest*
dreams of waking to the sudden

gust of drumming crow-black wings,
    the terror of my final breath
        cut short, a door slamming
    open on unfathomable dark –
never have I met whatever

held those rime- and brine-masked
    men in its piercing grip. *This must*
        be the end! they surely cried,
    relieved to find deliverance at last
from relentless shramming cold;

their voices lost to the vast emptiness
        of those North Atlantic floes, what
            else could they have wished except
        to be borne away in that heaven-sent
bone- and marrow-harrowing grasp?

O mortal grief! Could any soul
        survive intact when that screeching
            creature shivered with its saving
        grace their prayer for a swift demise?
O pale prospect of our disbelief!

Kallos. The Greek word for Beauty. From whence
Callisto. Calliope. The fine art
of uncial calligraphy, too. And hence
that Hellenic term conscripted to thwart
skeptics of the latest development
in the field of "photogenic drawing."
Calotype. Meaning Beautiful Imprint.
A new way of seeing. Or of showing.

Or of knowing the world through a picture
in duotone shades. What a poet moved –
"Beauty is truth, truth beauty" – Talbot proved
on the page in *The Pencil of Nature.*
A latent image fixed for evermore.
That moment captured in "The Open Door."

Outside another storm is howling; more
terrific than the one a poet heard
so many years ago, this tempest's roar
has loosened like a pickaxe the mortared
brick of faith. No master mason, I shore
up with doubtful timber – knotty, tortured
slabs of dim thought – the burden-bearing wall
of overwrought belief. It may yet fall.

On nights like this I shudder when, resigned
to fitful rest (at best), I rise to gaze
upon seraphic forms. Sprawled in purblind
bliss – so seemingly immune to my malaise –
those shadowy innocents call to mind
pale plastercast cherubs psaltering praise
from vaulted heights: rapture in high relief,
keystone rosettes in overarching grief.

Faultless harbingers of redeeming grace,
or heralds of the firmament's collapse?
Against the dark, my smarting eyes retrace
an archived image of nave, transept, apse –
a cathedral's heart – ravaged by the race
of wildfire over oak and stone. Perhaps
the answer lies buried in smoke-stained panes,
a sharded puzzle in rubbled remains.

Faith of my father, assuage my despair!
(Once, he saw in the glinting gilt-framed glass
on a print – *The Holy Family*, I swear –
his infant son falling, a hurtling mass,
and leaping caught him at the bottom stair.)
My daughters! Heaven forbid that I pass
disquiet to you. Pray that I root out
relics of hope from black ruins of doubt.

The book's epigraph, from Horace, translates as: "But if you place me among the lyric bards, / I shall touch the stars with my exalted head."

The epigraph to "Part I: Transmigration" is from a seventeenth-century Irish poet; it is translated thus by Michael Hartnett in *Haicéad* (Gallery Books, 1993): "When I'm awake I am in France; / asleep, I'm in my native land. / I love my vigils less and less – / yet sleep feeds my wakefulness."

"Stopping in Rock Barra": *Tempus edax rerum* comes from Ovid, *Metamorphoses*, 15, 234: "Time devours all things." The Delphic stump refers to the much-sung source of oracular knowledge in Greek mythology.

"The Death of Milton Acorn": the story of Jack Dale appears in F. H. MacArthur's *Legends of Prince Edward Island*.

"Whoso Pulleth Out This Sword": the title of this poem is borrowed from the inscription on the famous "sword in the stone" in Sir Thomas Malory's *Morte d'Arthur*.

"The Field": "Naming . . . is the love-act and its pledge" is borrowed from Patrick Kavanagh's poem "The Hospital."

"After Akhmatova": this poem derives from a stanza by Russian poet Anna Akhmatova.

"Metamorphoses": the epigraph to this poem, from Ovid's *Metamorphoses*, 12, 394, translates as: "if indeed we grant beauty to that tribe [i.e., Centaurs]." The story of Ixion is recounted most graphically in Pindar's *Pythian Ode* 2.

"The Miracle": the epigraph is borrowed from the "Circe" episode of James Joyce's *Ulysses*. While the incident referred to in this poem is usually associated with Franz Joseph Haydn's Symphony 96 in D major, first performed in London in 1791 and now known generally as "The Miracle," it actually occurred during a performance of Symphony 102 in B flat on 2 February 1795.

"Grappelli": French-born jazz violinist Stéphane Grappelli (1908-1997) is best-known for his recordings with legendary guitarist Django Reinhardt in the Quintet of the Hot Club of France.

"Paganini": this poem engages with both the myth and the reality of Italian violin virtuoso Niccolò Paganini (1782-1840).

"Reading Mandelstam": this poem engages with a lyric by Russian poet Osip Mandelstam. "Homer may nod" glances at Horace's *Ars Poetica*, 359: "*Indignor quandoque bonus dormitat Homerus.*"

"'They Became Mermaids'": this poem reworks a tale in F. H. MacArthur's *Legends of Prince Edward Island*; the epigraph is from Seamus Heaney's poem "Bogland."

"The Test of the Bow": Irish fiddler Michael Coleman (1891-1945) emigrated from County Sligo to New York City in 1918. His recordings continue to influence fiddlers on both sides of the Atlantic.

"After Looking Into R. J. O'Duffy's *Historic Graves in Glasnevin Cemetery* (1915)": the epigraph is borrowed from the "Hades" episode of James Joyce's *Ulysses*. The poem remembers Seumas O'Kelly, author of the fine Irish short story "The Weaver's Grave."

"As in Wild Earth a Grecian Vase": the title of this poem is borrowed from the closing lines of Padraic Colum's poem "A Poor Scholar of the 'Forties" – "Years hence, in rustic speech, a phrase, / As in wild earth a Grecian vase!" The Irish phrase *An Lár* translates as "City Center" – i.e., the center of Dublin.

"After Viewing David Blackwood's *Lost Party at Sea: The Sign*": this poem responds to a print by Newfoundland-born artist David Blackwood.

"The Pencil of Nature": this poem responds to William Henry Fox Talbot's pioneering work in photography in the late 1830s/early 1840s – specifically, his limited edition series (and later book) of "photogenic drawings" entitled *The Pencil of Nature*. "The Open Door" is one of his best-known calotypes.

ACKNOWLEDGMENTS

Acknowledgment is given to the following journals in which some of the poems in this book first appeared:

The Antigonish Review:	"Local Matters"
Canadian Literature:	"Fox Tongs," "A Poem Leaves No More Mark," "'They Became Mermaids'"
Crab Orchard Review:	"East Side Story"
Dalhousie Review:	"Dark Horses," "Stopping in Rock Barra"
The Fiddlehead:	"A Bicycle Built for Two," "The Fixed Link"
Kansas Quarterly/ Arkansas Review:	"Transmigration," "Auguries," "Valediction"
The Nashwaak Review:	"Cormorants," "The Field," "After Akhmatova"
The New Quarterly:	"Some Days, Paradise," "The Origin of Species," "Reading Mandelstam," "Russian Wedding," "*Bois d'Arc,*" "After Viewing David Blackwood's *Lost Party at Sea: The Sign*"

Poet Lore:	"Exile"
Poetry Ireland Review:	"South Boston Pier (1896)," "Cattle Crossing at Argyle Shore," "Thanksgiving," "The Test of the Bow," "As In Wild Earth a Grecian Vase," "A Prayer for My Daughters"
Pottersfield Portfolio:	"The National Dream," "I Could Be Tempted"
Queen's Quarterly:	"Bloodlines"
The Recorder:	"Dowry," "After Looking Into R. J. O'Duffy's *Historic Graves in Glasnevin Cemetery* (1915)," "*Tempus Edax Rerum*"
Verse:	"On Unquity Road," "What Really Matters," "Redemption"
Windsor Review:	"A Fiddler's Share," "Apologia"

Thanks to the St. Botolph Club Foundation for a grant-in-aid supporting the writing of this book

Thanks to the W. B. Yeats Society of New York for recognizing "Dowry" in its Annual Poetry Competition, 1999

The following poems were written *In Memoriam*:

"War Stories"   *i.m. Capt. James DeCoste (1956-1993)*

"Early"   *i.m. Allan Trenouth (1956-1997)*

"Close to Death"   *i.m. Seamus Crawford (1958-1988)*

The following poems were written in dedication:

"Bloodlines" *for Leah*; "South Boston Pier (1896)" *for Shaun & Dorothy*; "Cattle Crossing at Argyle Shore" *for Taine & Joe*; "Stopping in Rock Barra" *for Walter*; "The Death of Milton Acorn" *for Greg*; "Thanksgiving" *for Michael & Laura*; "Some Days, Paradise" *for Joe*; "After Akhmatova" *for Cathleen*; "A Bicycle Built for Two" *for Kathy & Chris*; "The Fixed Link" *for Carolyn & Marty*; "Reading Mandelstam" *for Laura & Joachim*; "Dowry" *for Joan & Danny*; "East Side Story" *for Brendan*; "Tempus Edax Rerum" *for Benedict Kiely*; "The Pencil of Nature" *for Fionán*